light

This book is the first in the Brainchild Award Series

light
paintings and poems by Celia Wesle

*To my friend Barbara
with warm regards
Celia Wesle*

Adonis Designs Press

Cover painting by Celia Wesle
"Checks" 1994; oil 6" x 8"

Copyright © 2007 by Celia Wesle
All rights reserved

Adonis Designs Press
P.O. Box 202
Chatham, Illinois 62629

Edited by Anita Stienstra
Front Cover Design by Carol Manley
Book Design produced by Carol Manley,
Celia Wesle, and Anita Stienstra
Published using technology and distribution
channels of LuLu Press

Manufactured in the United States of America

ISBN 978-0-6151-7659-8

Table of Contents

Introduction——Carol Manley

Blue——Chapter One

Light— My Totem	2
A Moment in Time When the World Was Perfect	3
Body Strength	4
Making Patterns	5
Weaving	6
Tribute to Andrews	7
Ten Speed	9
Holy Day	10
Intimacy	11
Phenyl Ethylamine	12
The Boy	13
Dear Donitza,	14
Powerful Words	15
Breakfast	16
Spring and Heading South in Illinois	17
Autumn and Heading South in Illinois	18
72	20
In Lincoln Library	21
Scalzo, the Artist	22
Eyes	23
Lions	24
The Only White Face at McDonald's	25
9/12	26
From the Sky	27
Final Check	29

Red——Chapter Two

Walk to School	32
What I Have Learned	33
Stay, Babies, Stay	34
American Meditation	35

Divine Feminism	37
Clue for Visiting Preacher	38
Didn't Recognize Sex	39
Engagement	40
Passion	41
The Chase	42
Pets	43
I Hear Her	44
Looking Through	45

Orange——Chapter Three

The Bath	48
At My Address	49
Water	50
At the Stove	51
Power	52
Boiled Oat Bran	54
Saturday Evening Meal	55
Friday 6:30 P.M. December	56
Thursday 10:30 A.M.	56
In the Bedroom	57
Room at the Back	58
Snow Angels	59
Homemade Soup	60
Hunger	61
At the Board	63

Green——Chapter Four

10–19–99	66
Green	67
Gentle Mental Cruelty	68
Please Don't Understand	69
The Decades	70
Self-Respect	71
Diabetes	72

Error	73
Illinois Green	74
Walking to My Car	75
Quiet Companionship	76
House Plants	77
Come Out	79
Hanging Plant	80
Listen	81

Brown——Chapter Five

Lovely	84
Spiritual Rejuvenation	86
At the Nursing Home	87
A New Stage	88
Marie Franciska Kretschmer	90
Crone Stage	91
Till Dying Day	92
At the End of My Arms	93
Art Class at the Senior Citizen's Center	94
Outside the Senior Citizen's Center	95
Only Elderly, Not Old	96
It's a Sweet Life	98
Lips	99
Thoughts at the Health Club	100
Rhythmic	101
Final Request	102

Introduction by Carol Manley

Celia Kreschmer Wesle is an elegant, graceful woman. I've had the pleasure over the years of hearing her read her poems, one or two at a time, in living rooms and public buildings around town. Now, with this collection all in hand at once, I've had the rare opportunity to see the world as Celia sees it. It's a gentle, sensual world of light and color.

Light is the overriding theme of these poems: sunlight rippling through water, the multiple meanings of headlights and tail lights in the night, the blinking eyes of mechanical devices when the house has been put to bed, the green eyes of a friendly young man on Saint Patrick's day. When, in a rare moment of irritability, she chastises the moon it is for only reflecting the sun, having no light of its own.

But these are not esoteric, day-dreamy poems. She is continually, beautifully present in the world. From the "Moment in Time When the World Was Perfect" where she describes a Mary Cassatt-like scene of being bathed as a child, to a graceful descent in a later age down the grand staircase at Lincoln Library, Celia is comfortably conscious in her own body. From the "kick-kick-kick" of grandchildren in the swimming pool to the tilt of a dentist's chair, riding in trucks and trains, and even in the act of writing poetry when "eyes survey what quickens [the] heart" the body is in motion.

In perfect simple lines throughout the poems, she isolates sensations: bare feet on carpet, chocolate melting on the tongue, a fast-food breakfast sitting "heavily in [her] gut," rhythmic rocking in a porch swing.

In the wistful "Dear Donitza," the purity of the scene ("fragrant lilacs…in a beige bowl" and an empty cane bottom chair) is reminiscent of William Carlos Williams as it paints the image without wasting a word.

"Ten Speed," "Tribute to Andrews," and "The Boy" deftly define relationships and loss. But always, throughout these poems, there is light. In "9/12" her unique sensibility and her best poetic devices resolve the horror of 9-11 into the reflection of red and white stripes on blue water. "As I approach/the reflection recedes./All I can do is look up/and feast on the brilliant colors/hanging above./My body is left untouched/wet in the pale blue."

This is grace. This is Celia.

Chapter One
Blue

"Niranjan" 2007; oil 34" x 45"

Light— My Totem

Sunlight
Sunlight reflected
Sunlight through leaves
Gorgeous forest
Light coming through jewels
Diamond brilliance
Reflections from my ruby
That circle of emeralds my
    mother gave me
Colored goblets on the
    window sill
Quartz crystal on my table
One hundred watts
    in all sockets
Sunlight on freshly fallen snow
Moonlight on the wavy lake
Immersed in shimmer
Summer in the pool
Surrounded by glimmer
Dancing under the disco ball
Always wear a transparent stone.
Always wear a ring as totem.

A Moment in Time
When the World Was Perfect

I'm two years old
sitting in a galvanized tub
on the kitchen table.
The water is comfortably warm.
Mother washes me
with a soft fragrant washcloth.
Rinses slowly,
saucepans of water
are poured over my shoulders.
I'm gently lifted
onto a towel,
another is wrapped around me.
I am patted until I'm dry.
A soft garment
clean smelling like the sun
is slipped over my head
and my whole body is happy.
We are in a sunny room
together. No one interrupts.

Body Strength

Poetry requires
the least physical effort
of all the arts,
not even a novel-sized
manuscript to transport,
no instrument to
lift into sound,
no large sheets of
paper or canvas
to raise into place,
no tubes or buckets
of paints to work open,
or brushes to choose from.
Dancing and even singing
require many deep breaths.
Instead, here I stand.
My eyes survey
what quickens my heart.
My mind
clickety-clicks
and the pencil moves.
Oh my soul!

Making Patterns

Up they go
sideways and over
caning a chair.

Round and
over the finger
curling my hair.

Dot, dot, powder base
under my eyes
hiding the age.

Sprinkle around
the black olive slices
on the pizza.
When baked,
eat three per bite.

Blow, whoo-whoo-whoo-whoo-whoo
out with
the night-time air.
Suck up
whu-whu-whu-whu-whu
Yoga morning freshness.

Reach and pull
kick-kick-kick-kick
Reach and pull
kick-kick-kick-kick
I tell my grandchildren
as I float them
in the pool.

Rhythm of life,
repetition
of motion;
I sit on my
porch swing
and think.

Weaving

I.
The weaver leans forward,
shoots the shuttle of woof
between the two warp rows.
Arms stretch for catch and return.

II.
Cloth World is a
universe of choices.
I ask the saleslady, "Where
do you keep the darning cotton?"
"Darning cotton?" she asks, puzzled.
I say, "Yes, thread to darn socks."
She shakes her head,
"We wouldn't have anything like that."

III.
Sister Honora, sewing class.
How to weave a cross,
in and out, back and forth
darning stockings.
I felt connected
with my great, great grandmothers
who lived in German houses
hinged at one corner
to move in large looms.

IV.
I choose not to give up
those pleasures of vision and motion:
there are holes to be filled!
My friend has punctured
two new pairs of socks.
I buy light gray embroidery
thread, instead.
My weaving will be on view
from his open-toed Birkenstocks.

Tribute to Andrews

Spring prairie drive,
between tree skeletons
on either side
crested with
whispers of leaves.
Whistling breezes
through open windows
raise the pitch of
ardent conversation
by two retired teachers
who never give up:
educational problems,
substitute teaching,
expertise in handling
the tough ones.

The principal says
"You're going
to really
like these kids;
they're the kind
you're good with."
Just because
no one else is?

"Hey, send me
some of the other kind!"
Cooperative ones
who want to learn.

With goof-offs
strategy is simple:
have a temper,
say what you mean,
mean what you say,
but have no
meanness in you:
the professional way.
Many students
look back
with fondness.

School year almost over.
Leaves will grow
and spread out,
cover the branches.
Then blossoms.
Then fruit.

Ten Speed

His icon, the bike,
sits along the windows
of the living room,
never touched—
unless the hired girl
dusts the fenders—
except when Flim-Flam,
the kitty, perches
on the high seat,
studies the sparrows
through the glass.

Those were pre-emphysema days,
when the body was wiry
      and able
        and tough
and could rise to the occasion
with skill and grit
win first place in the
state senior triathlon.

The studio represents HIM:
his fine exhibition photography,
favorite books, magazines,
articles, letters,
jazz tapes and disks
played daily,
videos of him
telling stories
and doing theater.

"This is ME, the artist,"
says the room.

"I can't get my breath.
Sometimes I think
I'm gonna die,"
says the man.

Holy Day

I met a young man
with St. Patrick's Day eyes
in a bookstore coffee shop.
I nestled in a brown
leather sofa facing
a fireplace blazing,
reading a purse-battered
New Yorker.
He spoke first:
"I never knew anyone
who read that."
In his hands was the open
"Do What You Love
and the Money Will Follow."
His eyes reflected his
green sweatshirt.
It was the Saint's Day.

Intimacy

His wrist rests on my temple,
his finger on my lip,
my hair touches his shirt front,
I look at his eyes but
they are focused elsewhere.
I swallow.
He smells nice:
no strong aftershave,
fierce antiseptic: just clean.
His hand brushes against my nose,
I feel a breeze blowing on my chin.
He lowers my back,
I hear water gurgling
I look at the blue dapple-painted wall
and float in its clouds.
One shoe has fallen off,
the other still hangs
on the tip of my toe.
My palms rest flat on my thighs.
I reflect: a 15-year relationship.
I hear whirring sounds,
I taste a mouthful of water
from a little blue cup.

His black-gray beard moves
as my dentist says,
"See you next week."

Do I love him? Of course.
How else could I bear
to have him so close,
his hand in my mouth.
But, it's a secret from him
and everyone else— except you
and you, and you.

Phenyl Ethylamine

Her dentist
would wince
if he knew her
newest sin since
seeing him last.
She pops a disk
of that dark brown
all-time goodie
on her tongue
to slowly melt
as she goes to sleep.

Scientists have found
that chocolate
will create
a bodily chemical
akin to sex,
a naturally released,
relaxing after-effect
of affectionate
passion.

So, before she
gives up her body
to Morpheus
she needs
at least a
semblance
of love.

The Boy

He was his mother's
and his aunties'
precious boy— grown up,
and when he
presented a dandelion, I smiled
in gracious gratitude,
but I would have
preferred a gardenia.

We took our children, cut down a tree
and decorated the branches.
When he gave me
a can of tuna
wrapped in Christmas paper,
I smiled at his playfulness,
but he knew
I would have preferred
a jewel or book.

He was a
me-me-mine fellow,
fearful of generosity
as a sign of
having been seduced,
being taken advantage of,
careful to be evasive and stingy
especially to someone
who had been loving.

He said,
"I want to have you,"
but I left
feeling no more valued by him
than were his dusty, already clipped
rat-packed newspapers,
which he wanted even more
and had till he died.

Dear Donitza,

Am sitting opposite
the cane bottomed chair
you used last time
at my kitchen table.
In my mind's eye
I see you there,
and wish it was real,
and you could smell
the fragrant lilacs I have
right there
in a beige bowl,
and chat with me.

Affectionately,

Celia.

Powerful Words

Perky red bow tie
under young wide smile
in glowing face,
the Steak and Shake waitress
leans toward me,
answers my question
with assurance:

"YOU CAN HAVE ANYTHING
YOU WANT
TWENTY-FOUR HOURS A DAY."

My throat chokes,
voice quivers
"I'll have the…"
Will my tears spill out
before I can finish?
"…#6 breakfast special."

Author's note: I was driving south after visiting several days with my mother in a Wisconsin nursing home, thinking about her decline and all my other problems. I took a break in a restaurant hoping it was not too late in the day to have a breakfast. Her words moved me.

Breakfast

Thank you
Cosmic Birth-er
for the sun
in this orange
I chew.
It descends
through my throat,
past my heart
to become beams that
radiate throughout me
everywhere:
brain labyrinth
fingertips
hip cells.
I fill with sunshine
and minerals.

Spring and Heading South in Illinois

The truck rolls
through Shawnee Forest.
Spring rains
arouse daffodils,
grace with yellow faces.
It doesn't ping
as loudly
on the glass
when it lets up.
Brown brooks bounce
around rocks and twigs,
gurgle a laugh!
"We don't care," they say,
"if we're not clear and fair
like Missouri Ozark
pebble-bedded streams.
We're richly colored
like Illinois' good soil."

Autumn and Heading South in Illinois

Past the sorghum field
toward Highway 15,
east through Beaucoup
toward Ashley,
Hardees' sausage platter
sits heavily in my gut,
the last quarter of coffee
on the dashboard.
We ride without speaking,
partly awake.
Turn at Nashville.
Back there in Elton Hazlitt State Park
the thunder and lightning
had sent power
through the tent walls.
Heavy rainfall outside.
Glad for my friend and his dog.
This morning the clouds
are low and black.
A strip of yellow brightness
just below the far tree line,
then a row of dark green
coming toward us,
then straw-colored fields.
Cut corn stalks with
an occasional oil pump.

A small bird flock
banks and turns across the highway
toward some indifferent cows.
A farmhouse near the road
has orange tapes

(replacing yellow bows?)
wound around its porch columns.
A black fluttering ghost shape
hangs over its steps
for the all souls' season.
The horizon highlight
has turned peachy.
The black clouds
have developed silver-gray edges.
Another flock of birds
passes in front
and we drive underneath.
Many others sit on the telephone wires
warming themselves on the talk.
Beneath them the swollen water
flows along the gullies
in the green roadside grass.
The truck heater works well.
I rouse to the day.

72

Seventy-two
Oriental snuff bottles
      in rows
cover the colored poster
from my Hawaiian friend.
Jade, alabaster,
carved, blown, painted
works of art
honor the sneeze.

A hearty breath
powers a head orgasm,
sends the body
over the top to release
and statement.

Is it spring spores,
July blooms,
or household dust
that runs my drip,
and without beauty
or intention
blows into a hefty shriek.

The thrill is there, but
I wish for the elegance.

In Lincoln Library

To allay old age
breathlessness and fatigue
she chooses the effortless
claustrophobic lift
to do her art and music
book business upstairs.

Then she turns to the center
of the big room
where a huge skylight
illumines the broad stairway.
She pauses at the top,
one day a queen
another a bride
in long jeweled
but weightless garments,
sweeps airborne down
slowly and
majestically.

Scalzo, the Artist

Lillian likes
women's bodies
as only a woman can
respectful, frank
joyous, gentle
probably mindful
of her own.

Cloaked madonnas
ethnic dancers
hoop-skirted fashion
paint, stitchery
but best of all
shape and surface
nude and enameled.

Panel of seven
copper cut
bride white
pregnant bare
hour-glass black
blue high waist
defined nipples
spill over.

Ten lovely times
around the room
small single
female forms
glow from
glass melted
contours shaped
by tiny grains of color.

Five friends
pause in gallery
look and write.

Eyes

Round or almond shaped,
piercing blue, sleepy.
They all look at me.
What do they see?
Where can I hide?
Go out in the country
where they are fewer.

Sitting around the table
in the farm kitchen,
through the window
someone sees a red taillight.
All conversation stops.
Speculation starts.

Lions

The grand foreign
fountain splashes.

Drops of water
mixed with air and
sunshine sparkle.

Bavarian sculptures
shoot out arching streams
from the mouths of
frogs and turtles.

What are those big cats
doing in all that wetness?

The Only White Face at McDonald's
(haiku)

Gray	skies	overhead
Like	metallic	reflection
Steel	City	blackness.

Author's note: Took an exit with my car into Gary, Indiana— Steel City— for a break at a McDonald's. When I sat in the busy restaurant, I was startled to realize that I was the only white person. The day was very dark. There was smokiness all around.

9/12

The intense sun
comes through the huge
American flag
spread over the wall of windows
at the Health Club
on September twelfth
and shines its colors
on the swimming pool water.

I wade toward it
hoping to be encircled
by red and white moving stripes
to wander into the deeply bright blue field,
to have its stars bump against my wet skin.

As I approach
the reflection recedes.
All I can do is look up
and feast on the brilliant colors
hanging above.
My body is left untouched
wet in the pale blue.

From the Sky

Lunar power,
full round being,
don't hang over us
sending your reflected sun
onto our skin and hair.
Old and new tales warn of
lunacy promoted,
of hospitals
regularly agitated
during certain
of your phases.

Let us sit instead
on a porch swing
covered overhead,
sheltered
from which
we can watch
the moving leaf
moon-shadows
over there.
Or, on the open beach
put your arms around me,
pull me close,
face the bonfire
so that its red and yellow
heat and glow hit us
to reduce the impact
from that large white circle above
and its path
shimmering incessantly
straight at us
across the water.

"Mother and Infant" 1949; oil 14" x 20"

Final Check

Swing around the banister,
bare feet feel carpet
then hardwood.
Fingers jiggle locks
on the doors
to the night.
Push the switches
for basement darkness.
Striped by blinds,
the security lights
from the deck
are reflected
in the large
Jacuzzi mirrors
through glass doors
into the dim, quiet room
through which I walk.

All around are eyes
blue, red, even green ones
following my moves:
electric signals telling time,
availability and control
of music, VCR, cooking,
house temperature.

I pass among them
and return
up the carpeted stairs
to the sleeping grandchildren.

Chapter Two
Red

"Painting of Collage" 1995; oil 24" x 36"

Walk to School

She carefully sets
the long, bright yellow
loosely knit scarf
to look tossed
around her waving
yellow hair,
blue eyes bright.

Last year she
bundled as usual
against the Wisconsin cold
with lined hood
over wool cap,
heavy mittens, thick boots,
books hugged to her chest.
Nature had first loosed the lining of her womb
four years ago,
but now she blooms.

She's fifteen.
Her body glows.
Her face sparkles.
She so warms
the atmosphere
around her head
that those yellow
strands of yarn
one square inch apart
catch and hold
against the snowflakes
a magic winter heat,
and she floats cozy
down the street
and feels pleased and pretty.

What I Have Learned

I should have kissed him,
leaned forward
(maybe slipped my hands over
his shoulders for balance),
laid my lips on his,
moved those lips
to show I'm alive.

But the information I had
(stories Mother read aloud)
was that the princess waited,
she even slept,
until HE came
and did the leaning.

Oh, what I missed!
The hours I talked
(words hold bodies apart).
No brothers or peer cousins
to realize the true nature
of the male who wants
a signal, a come-on.

If only I'd leaned forward
and laid my lips on his!

Stay, Babies, Stay

Such pain;
ears hear others' moans,
groans and shrieks;
the doctor speaks
with calm:
"It would help
if you would
stop shaking."
If only I could.

I quake with fear.
The bag is cut.
The water released.
They breathe.
Juliana dies.
Janet survives.
Thirty years ago.
My hands still shake.

American Meditation

Autos
in lines
motors idling,

Driver
patient
leaning on elbows,

Window
rolled down
where arm rests,

Wax
scribbled
on windshield,

Clue
for washers:
do chassis bath,

Salt
dims the
colored metals,

Snow
finally
melted and gone,

Sun shining
we float into
space-out time,

Lines
lengthen
three times nine,

Cars
slowly
creep forward,

Shine,
emergence,
reverie ended.

Divine Feminism

Life
kisses
lover.

Life
births
babies.

Life
gives breast
to infant.

Life
teaches
without censure.

Life
grows
and changes.

Life
avoids
machismo.

Life
listens
and blesses.

Clue for Visiting Preacher

Ancient Middle Eastern
male nomads
can be excused
for imagining
their vengeful God
as a "He"
but we
know God is Love.

Love is an "It"
God is Truth,
Beauty, Good,
all gender-free.
In fun, to make
the point, we
sometimes call IT, "She."

Eternal Spirit
most highly venerated
all pervasive IT,
we honor thee!

Didn't Recognize Sex

Had no male hero
in my life
till I moved from home.
Wonder why.

Slight impact
from Nelson Eddy—
a tall, singing blond
like my father—
which figures, and
Tyrone Power–cute.

In the Beloit College
campus art hall
a bigger than life-size statue
of Michelangelo's David,
my first male nude,
aside from the crucified Jesus
(somewhat covered with a floating
 sheer scarf)
on my classroom walls.

Visited David often,
excited and thrilled
by the lovely physical warmth
filling my torso.
Not a living person
but so what…

Engagement

That piece of carbon, pressurized
in platinum holder, glorified
twinkles up at me
like his eyes, happily.

He's a younger man, of seventy-three
"Go for it," they say to me.
I go, and come.
Heart filled with sun.

Passion

"Hallelujah," the choir sings,
"He's turned my mourning
into dancing again."
Whatever inspires:
Jesus,
dumpling soup,
a lover,
sun through the leaves
I encourage joy.
Whatever healthy turns you on,
Hallelujah!

The Chase

Big horse fly,
why
do you zoom
varoom
around my
room?

It's winter.
Was your egg
under a splinter
on my baseboard,
then furnace-warmed,
central-heating hatched?

Can't catch you
though I follow
from this room to that
poised with swatter
ears and eyes alert
with murder in my heart.

Pets

Joan thinks
I do not like dogs
like her big
black
puppy.

I told her,
I like dogs,
but I don't encourage them
because I don't know
how to tell them to stop.

I don't like them to leap on me,
to slobber my hands,
or sniff my crotch.

However
I love to have
any living thing
lie on and warm my feet,
lovingly look into my eyes,
place head on my knee.
Living contact:
not living dominance.

I Hear Her

Clickity click
like high heels
coming across
the linoleum floor.
It's not
a short-stepping
young lady
but an old dog,
with nails rather long,
come to find crumbs
under the kitchen table.

Looking Through

Wee life things
carcassed into
tiny feather fans
across my windshield
are opaque shapes
between transparent
crystal-like
clinging raindrops:
death on the highway.

Chapter Three
Orange

"Valentine Collage" 1960; 28" x 11"

The Bath

A pale warm skin sack
more beautiful than a
Hallmark gift bag
(has curving contours)
holds her
valuable innards.
She lowers it gently
into blossom fallout,
daughter having moved
the green geranium boxes
next to the tub on the
blue bathroom window sills.

She floats with the
soft salmon, red
pink petal disks—
a Hawaiian forest pool.
The Dove-scented washcloth
strokes her surface,
grown long ago
from ectomorph cells
like her ears and brain,
and she hears and thinks
freshly with sensitized skin.

At My Address

My home.
My own
happy walls
Mein Heim,
big windows
of sunshine,
at best
give rest
where I say,
"So glad
I can stay
today— not
have to go
anywhere,"
by someone
who likes
to run
around town.
My rooms
let me down
only when
maintenance
confounds me.
Smudged walls,
faded carpet,
broken water heater,
overflowing
book shelves.
I slowly solve
my problems,
try to keep my thoughts
from pushing—
my sense
of perfection
kept in its place.

I am rewarded
with contentment.

Water

Large cobalt blue
glass pitcher,
Bonnie and Charlie's gift
sits in my
kitchen sink,
fills up for
humidifier maintenance.

I stand by,
drink ice water.

At the faucet
it splashes and sings
in rising pitch,
hits E.
I sense it's full,
set down my mug,
tend to it.

At the Stove

How
can a dead cow
smell so good?

This
vacillating vegetarian
went back to bride-time,
used an old favorite recipe.
That was another world:
a small Iowa college town.
The grocer said
he'll order leeks for me
if I buy the whole crate—
no one else would know
how to use them.

Now-a-days I see
fresh oriental vegetables
on supermarket racks.
I meet people
(though not the checkers)
who know a kohlrabi.

It's been awhile
since I've stood in my kitchen
and fixed beef.

Power

My power
manifests
when I
pay my bills,
put on paper
the letters
I've been talking
in my head,
send them out
with articles
I've put aside
for my daughters.
My Power
manifests
when I put on the table
the vegetables
I've yearned for
and the bread
I sometimes bake,
when the colors
and compositions
in my mind's eye
are down on paper
and canvas—
and framed, even,
and submitted to shows,
when the photos
I've taken materialize magically
through the liquid
in the developer tray,
when the poems
I write are typed
on a computer,
I have yet to select
and buy,

and submitted for publication.
I feel power
when the dust is gone
and the furniture
and glass shine,
when closets,
drawers and garage
are orderly,
when my fingers
are nimble again
with guitar strings
and piano keys,
when my bulbs
are planted, when I've figured out
how to adjust
the answering machine,
the VCR, the microwave.
I feel power
when I've decided
on the color
of new carpeting
and arranged to
have it put in.

Why are all
these thoughts so depressing?
At least I got
my library loans
returned on time,
and my laundry is done,
and I got in today's water aerobics.

And
I wrote another poem.

Boiled Oat Bran

Were
you
tasting good,
I would
be eating
eagerly,
too
quickly for
thorough chewing,
too
quickly
for optimal health—
reluctantly yearned for,
ruefully worked for,
hopefully
worth having.

Go
on
grinding away
fat globules,
scouring
around in arteries,
coddling
the colon,
patting
the conscience
with
"Good Girl."

Now,
down
the toilet
with you,
swirl away.
I've had
enough
of you
today!

Saturday Evening Meal

Barley with bay leaf,
fresh tomatoes,
lambs quarters from
my weeds garden
stewed together
with tasty salts.
Occasionally swigs
of my olive martini
make the green world
around my glass
patio table
swirl slightly.
My wet swim suit
cools my flesh
with memories of
blue water down the hill
in gracefully shaped pool.
The round sun
sparkles between the
moving maple leaves.
The world hums
as light reflects
from the huge lawn.

Friday 6:30 P.M. December

Leona put lights on
the lilac bush
red white
blue yellow green
(I see as I lean
against my kitchen sink)
bright on the
dark sky
above the low sunset.

Thursday 10:30 A.M.

The late morning sun
big, round, white
through the dark pine needles
sits on the peak
at the corner
of Leona's house
waiting for me
to see—
pause my bustling energy.

In the Bedroom

Colored transparent
glass flowers and leaves
hang from the curtain rod
of the wide window,
framed by white eyelet above,
yellow drapes swagged
with gold chains at the sides,
and eyelet half-curtains
pushed apart down below.

With a cheek on a
blue silky down pillow
I see horizontal brown leaves
outside, windblown,
gray sky behind them.
Yesterday I had rejoiced
as these same leaves
pointed sprightly
in all directions,
glowed clear yellow—
some especially bright
as sunlight permeated them
in patches here and there—
with beautiful blue
between the branches.
A bright red cardinal
comes to sit on the
suctioned, transparent
pocket of birdseed
against the pane.

There is so much
my eyes revel in.
I transfer the sight
to my inner eye,
let my lids close,
and ease into
my afternoon sleep.

Room at the Back

Yellow like sunshine
coarse weave drapes
open wide
at the south window,
short dotted Swiss
across the lower half
framing evergreen trees
outside.

Beyond the hanging plants
an old
round oak table
are sliding glass doors
that show maples and grass.

I think of my neighbor Diane
on the other side
of the north wall,
range, refrigerator,
and wall-long shelf
homemade by me
that holds pots and pans
over the cupboards.

Also a round decorative
Mexican plate
and a blue and white
round mandala
from an Icelander
using symbols for that culture.

Snow Angels

I look through
across tall frosted
wild weeds
on the other side of
my wide windows.
A bright white world
reflects energizing sunshine
throughout my cozy rooms,
glows from creamy walls,
chrome and gold frames,
jumps from one shiny
book jacket to another,
bounces onto goblets
in the breakfront and
makes alive the carpet color.
Angels blended into the
fuzzy snowy outdoors
lean close against
my windows, look through.
I say, "Welcome.
Come on in!"

Homemade Soup

vitamin juices
from recently living
growths
just briefly touched
with heat for
softer texture
in stainless steel
on electric range
(no dangerous rays)
snip a leaf from
big cauliflower bouquet
cut carrot coins
celery leaves
leek disks.

always start with
garlic and onion
in olive oil
add broccoli broth
from yesterday's lunch
half a tomato
left from supper
a few small
cubes of tofu
Britta filtered water.

black, round, spicy
peppercorns
I spit into the grass
like watermelon seeds
from where I sit
under the maple
in beautiful breezes
at my glass-topped
patio table.

Hunger

Yearning, desire, a
fire stuck in a spot.
Hot and chilled,
filled with needs.
Seeds of satisfaction and
interaction unsprouted.

Doubt relief will come:
some food or friend to
end the hollow feel, a
meal or hug or smile
while I wait and suffer.
Tougher than I guessed.

Blessed with time to endure,
perhaps to find a cure.

"Sioux City Alma" 1951; oil 8" x 10"

At the Board

Do you remember
pushing the pointed
tip of the hot iron
along the wavy lace
on the puffed sleeves
and round collars
of little girls' dresses?
Sister, here I am
gone to elderly
with a dripping nose.
I push the heat
into the scalloped edges
of the white and colored
cotton hankies
from the back of my drawer.
The collapsing soft paper
of modern invention is
no longer sufficient
on these wintery days.

Chapter Four
Green

"Growing" 1999; oil 10" x 7 3/4"

10-19-99

I adore
the brightness
of the sunshine
and the quietness
of the night.
Can I get both
at the same time?
Bright sunlight
bleaches out details.
Night hides them
in the shadows.
Peace of both
no interruptions
to my sensing
to my feeling
to my responding
to my reality
to my mindfulness
and meditation.
My eyes close.
With each extreme
I sink into peace.

Green

Trees, grass, river.
My eyes turn north,
south, east, west
up above and down below.
All verde
except for little
patches of pale
blue between branches.
Green for growth and health,
Midwest staying power,
sun energy with chlorophyll
rain for thirst.
I breathe deeply
and soak in the sight.

Gentle Mental Cruelty

It is the heart and mind
where the bruises don't show
for a while.

His impatient rolling eyes
belittle me to friends.
He turns away,
his back leaves the room
when I'm asked to sing.
His palm, on stretched-out arm,
faces me flat to shut me up
finish his "lecture," his "story."
No immediate response allowed.
I would be spoiling his evening
or anytime,
to make a remark
or ask a question
about our relationship.
"If you're going to be that way!"

The open, loving heart,
sharing its innards, wounded,
slowly closes its scarred edges.
The mind views the pain,
doesn't understand,
for a while.

Please Don't Understand

So fast,
placating,
without queries about
aspects of my thoughts,
without wondering
what I feel,
as if you cared.

Don't shut
me up by
saying only
"I understand."

The Decades

If the lace on the camisole
has loosened and frayed a bit,
do you in the 70's style
discard, make room for new?

Or, do you, in 30's style
slip on your silver thimble,
admire the shallow metal scrollwork
of plant forms circling
its dimpled top,
find cream colored thread,
a fine but big-eyed embroidery needle,
proceed to preserve in 90's
ecologically correct
recycling style,
and think as you stitch
about its effect
under your suits
below your neck
over your bosom?

Self-Respect

Who knows
and who cares
if I have
little rips
in my pastel green
cotton panties?

I do.
Can self-respect
be influenced
by so little?

Time to throw away,
also, the full slip
rarely worn
these slack days
and to shop
for new and renew
the glory of
my lingerie drawer.

Diabetes

Dear Insides,
beneath my epidermis,
through sinew,
under fat

Is the truth:
worn out isles,
weary pancreas
and liver— likely;

Oh orange-capped
Humulin of Lilly!
Will
I ever be through
with you?

How bittersweet
to hear him say,
"You are the sweetest person
I have ever known."

Error

The word won't go away.
My little computer
confounds my senses.
My blood runs
wasted, onto my
journal page.
So many errors
around, like my
swollen ankles.
Radiant health
my primary goal.
Floss, breathe deeply,
continue counting carbs,
and hydroflex.

Illinois Green

Two days more,
busy with tasks before
she goes to Greece.
But she takes time
to drive through
Washington Park.
What is the pull?

Illinois green,
I guess,
civilized city-park
restraint, and
a healthy lushness
old Hellas
may not have.

For a few weeks
she's trading
oxygen from leaves
for breezes over blue seas
coming through
broken temples and
around abandoned rocks,
silver-gray olive trees
slim, dark Cyprus—
or so travel books suggest.

She's saying, "So long."

Walking to My Car

Shaped and colored
like pale yellow mums,
the sky's reflection
flashes to me
from the car's rear window.
They're warm
sunset clouds,
small and puffy,
floating above
treetop stems.
Blue sky picture,
framed by blue car
in my deep green world.

Quiet Companionship

I play with my flowers.
Every morning I
look to see
how they are.
Sometimes they need unwinding.
Is the soil moist?
I lightly scratch
the hard brown bumps/bugs
from the stalks
and when my long
fingernail is filled,
flush the debris
down the sink.
The oxalis has many blooms,
which dry,
and I tweak them off.
These living entities
get my frequent
grooming and constant admiration.
Upon arising, I
walk along my sunny windows and
say my good morning to them.
I've brought in
some pink impatiens
and the forget-me-not plants
that I raised from seed
but have not yet bloomed.
Maybe they never will,
but they're here,
welcomed into my home
whose only other living thing
is me.

House Plants

A soundless "whoo-oo-oo-w-w."
Now I inhale.

Then a soundless "Ha-a-a-a-ah."
I bless you with my breath,
remembering the Creator
who breathes life into all.
With reverence,
dear Oxalis and Airplane,
I lean over you
breathe on you
groom and water you.
Here is my carbon dioxide
for your well-being.
I receive your oxygen.
Inhale.
We nourish each other.
We commune.
Hmn-n-n-n.

"Polka and Poochie" 2006; watercolor 15" x 11"

Come Out

"Come out,
come out,
wherever you are!"
Old lady
leans over
window sill and leafy plants,
looks intently
into each center.

Winter almost over
time for blossoms
blue, purple, pink
African violets.
She quietly calls
old hide-and-
go-seek chant
"Come out,
come out,
wherever you are!"

Hanging Plant

They flourish,
those shiny green leaves
births with reflection
on sprightly branches.
At least they seem so,
till I look
more closely.
Some are dead,
dried,
hanging brownish,
wrinkled.
Was it me
not providing enough water?
If so,
how did they determine
who was to live
and who was to go?
There is no pattern,
not all the tips or
not all the big,
old ones.
Did some say,
"I will release my life
for the welfare
of the whole?"
Did some say
"Not I, not I!
Why would I
do that?"
Sure, death
is part of having been alive,
but when or why
this or that one?
It makes no sense.

Listen

Let me
listen to the Silence
so I can hear
my house plants breathe.
So I can feel
my heart pump blood
up and down
my arms and legs.

Let me
ignore the radio and CDs
so I can concentrate
on the sun beams' energies.
Let me
listen to the silence
around me and you
so I can sense the joy
between us two.

Chapter Five
Brown

"Across" 1995; watercolor 7½" x 10"

Lovely

Dimple and pretty teeth,
genteel of manner
but dependable
and strong, slim
good cook and seamstress,
ideal old-fashioned wife
(wonderful present day person).
She would spontaneously
harmonize to his tenor
as they played zither
and guitar together.

My father adored her long
chestnut-brown braids,
brushed and rebraided,
wound after sleep
against the back of her head.
At his fervent request
she avoided the flapper cuts.
I remember the narrow
black velvet ribbon
tied around it daily
when I was little.
I would watch its dark
fuzzy texture bound by
tiny shiny satin edges
as her head moved.

They danced beautifully.

She was fun, wrote
amusing verses my sister and I
would recite for parties.
She liked the joyfulness
of religion and
depended on meditative prayers.

She saw my dad
as her handsome, gifted prince.
I asked her once
if Papa ever expressed
a desire to return to Germany.
She reflected a minute
then smiled and said,
"Nein, nie. Er wolte immer
sein wo ich bin."
No, never. He always wanted to be
where I am.

Spiritual Rejuvenation

Mother will be
ninety next month
her house is
suddenly so shiny.
She seems to have forgotten
her aching hip and back.
She touches her cheek
with a tender smile;
the new young priest
came to visit.

He stayed two hours.
He picked up
her wedding picture
again and again—
seeing the beautiful
regal lady
in 20's simple lace
next to the handsome tall blond
holding his top hat.

The former parish priest is gone.
"What do I need
with a bitter old man?"
She says to me,
her fingertips on her cheek
where her new visitor kissed her.
Having promised to
lead the rosary
at the funeral home
when the time comes
to maintain her honor
with her churchy relatives.

At the Nursing Home

Decaying flesh,
confused thoughts,
leaking orifices,
slumped settling bones—
sometimes spurs,
dimming eyes,
misjudged grasp,
faltering steps,
whimpering sounds,
begging dependency.

At best, aides
treat them like doll babies,
pull down their shirts,
wash between their legs,
roll up wet pads,
pull on new slacks,
ask, "Where does it hurt?"
gently comb pillow-flattened hair—
shape it around the face,
slip glasses onto nose.

Daughter comes,
pushes wheelchair out
into Indian summer air,
gathers apples
under the tree
and with a jack knife,
at the round patio table,
peels and slices.
Bees gather, buzz,
suck on cores.

A New Stage

I love my mother.
Have I known anyone longer?
Seventy-three years.
Can't imagine life without her
though I didn't
live my adult
life in her city.
Now I go to another state
to visit the nursing home
for three, four long
days every month.

Today she looked at me
thoughtfully and asked
"Bin ich deine Mutter?"
(Am I your mother?)
We have reached a new stage.
I answer her questions
and she nods.
We still talk and laugh
together about
the here and now:
the red velour jacket
I brought with the
longish matching skirt
to hang over her
amputated legs,
the manicure I give her,
things I read aloud.

She can describe,
when I ask,
the Kachelofen
in her birth house,
which heated the room,
was cooked on,
provided hot water.
And eine Ofenbank
where my great
grandmother liked to sit.
That was in Seitendorf,
Saxony, the town
entirely dug up
to make Polish coal mines.

She answers my questions
in entertaining detail
about very long ago.

Marie Franciska Kretschmer

Farewell, my Mama-Love,
goodbye weakened limbs,
loneliness, tiredness.
Tshuess to helplessness.

Greetings, freedom.
Hi, pure consciousness.
Welcome, beauty,
joy and Karl.

Born to life on
July 15, 1899.
Born to eternal life on
July 15, 1999.

Farewell, my one and only
Mama.

Crone Stage

Life's possibilities
shrink, drop away.
I will probably
never ski in the Alps,
be my country's president,
no chance again
to cradle my baby
against my heart.

Maybe never again
see the eyes sparkle
in a man fantastically
in love with me?

Oh, that is sad!

Till Dying Day

Mother Earth deserves
a healthy body
for her dust.
Good excuse!
So I pray, Eternal Spirit,
help me keep
this temple
fit and well.
Someday
may that I
finish my pattern
while active
on the square dance floor.
I'll drop
stretch out,
smile up.
Friends will circle around, "Oh!"
look down,
watch my eyes close,
bless my transition.

At the End of My Arms

These wonderful hands,
experienced fingers,
have plucked guitar strings,
peeled thousands of carrots,
bathed babies and children
gently, year after year,
they've painted pictures, embroidered,
built, loved, blessed.
They've written a million words.

Suddenly now they're so ugly.
Are these mine?
I notice in the mirror
large scattered brown spots,
thick pale blue veins,
stiff finger curled,
wrists gaunt, tumor lump
no watch can hide.

But the nails are shapely,
I paint them red!
And see here my loveliest:
diamonds,
a large amethyst,
some emeralds,
and waiting in my drawer
with color, light, fire
a great ruby!

Art Class at the Senior Citizen's Center

So much vital energy
in the air around me.
The room is drenched
with lifelong yearnings for beauty.
White, gray heads bend over
blue, black, beige rectangles of paper.
Fingers smudged in greens and magentas
hold pieces of pastels,
brush here and there,
make colored areas
that reflect back the life and sparkle
of azaleas and lemons
against draped olive velvet.
Fringes finger down the edge
of the card table.
Helen demonstrates:
pats the tan paper with green pigment
sharpens the yellow stick
and slides it along the oval shapes.
All the drawings differ
with personal views and thoughts.
Wonderful experiences.
The products are not
the goal, alone.

Outside the Senior Citizen's Center

In long row
red orange tulips,
stems evenly spaced,
stand straight there,
metal pole rises
up to limp flag.

Old lady below,
bent down over
green and yellow
grass and dandelions,
studies ground
around her feet
for four-leaf clover.

"If you believe—
it will be there,"
she tells me.
I wonder what
her big wish is.

Only Elderly, Not Old

She folds her fingers
into palms, presses
on knuckles for balance
to lift herself from the sofa,
like an ape
rather than the graceful swan
she used to be
with strong dancer's thighs
raising and lowering
at will, wherever.
Everything is effort.

Her bicycle, tennis racquet,
cross country skis
sit in the garage and
wait, maybe forever.
She cannot manage
to stand upright
at the cashiers'
leans across the counter,
rests on her elbows
till transaction complete.
Everything is effort.

She holds her fork
with a fist,
elbow out to steady
the lettuce.
Will it reach her mouth?

She sips the soup's tomato broth
from the edge
leaving the vege-
tables for an unliquid later.
Everything effort.

When no one is looking,
she raises the wires
holding her plastic teeth
with the tips of her thumbs,
so the tongue
can fish underneath
for the crumbs
pressing on her gums.
Everything effort.

It's a Sweet Life

I always used to want
to get very old,
to have many years
to appreciate the earth,
to feel its breezes
on face, in hair,
to submerge myself
in warm water,
to see the sun shine
through my windows,
to pull a cool arm
back under soft covers,
to be smiled at,
to be touched
to taste cherries.

Now I'm seventy-three, and
though all the above
still happen to me,
I also find it's
beginning to be unbearable, cells
gone awry on my leg,
fingers stiff and
writing ungraceful,
veins in my eyes
threatening sight,
syringe points my skin protests
four times daily,
legs and heart that can't express
my joy of dance.

I eat my broccoli
and drink my carrots,
I measure out and swallow
my food supplements,
I read many interesting books,
and I bravely keep my membership
in the polka club.

Lips

If I smiled only
ten times a day,
by now I would have
stretched the skin
on my lips over
two hundred sixty thousand times.

It is understandable then
that in five places
the edges have disappeared
between my lower lip
and the skin above my chin,
and the stretch marks,
three on the left side
two on the right,
go down and up in repose
and my lipstick runs the length
into my light skin.
So I put on collagen
anti-feathering complex
(small tube $19).

The truth is,
I smile at least
twice that often.

Thoughts at the Health Club

Being a
Ruben's woman
has been
a delight,
indolence,
rich food,
the power and joy
of moving my pounds,
throwing my
weight around
in actuality
sensing and flowing
with centrifugal force
from my own motion!

But
enough
is enough!
Do I have a choice of being svelte
again?
Will I return
to willowy-round—
my young and midlife
contour—
or just be an
old bag of bones
from reduced food,
increased exercise?

Well, work,
Muscles of Mine,
stretch away.
Who can say?

Rhythmic

Ripples across wet lake,
undulation over windy greases,
flutter in leaves up the tree,
layers of stratus-cumulous above
resemble
mature body surface
no longer smooth
with young skin on
arms, legs, waist, back.

Life shows itself
with different beauty.

Final Request

Aging,
worrying,
life's last hours.
How long
on the machine?
We respect
the energy
of crystals,
the emotional life
of house plants,
so
be patient
with me
as a vegetable.
Talk to me and
be not uneasy.
I will hear your voice
or sense your intent.
Tell me about
your days and
your nights.
Put into words
the mutual memories
you can recall.
I may very well
be aware.
Like me
like I am.
Don't sorrow

by comparing me
with who/what
I once was.
Be patient
with me
inert,
for I'm proud
to still be
hanging in there.

"Sister at the Piano" 1942; oil 16" x 20"